DATE DUE

DEMCO 38-296

NEWT

INSIDE THE REVOLUTION

NEWT

INSIDE THE REVOLUTION

Photographs by P. F. Bentley

on assignment for TIME magazine

Introduction by William F. Buckley Jr.

Captions by Karen Tumulty

**Quotations from the speeches and writings of
Speaker of the House Newt Gingrich**

AN EPICENTER COMMUNICATIONS BOOK

Rutledge Hill Press

Nashville, Tennessee

Created and Produced by

Epicenter Communications
Sausalito, California 94965

President, Epicenter Communications: Matthew Naythons, MD
Art Director: Alex Castro
Editor: Dawn Sheggeby
Director of Photographic Production: Peter Goggin
Assistant Editor: Katherine Withers
Copy Editor: Lisa Bornstein

Published in Nashville, Tennessee, by Rutledge Hill Press, Inc., 211 Seventh
Avenue North, Nashville, Tennessee 37219. Distributed in Canada by H.B.
Fenn and Co., Ltd., 1090 Lorimar Drive, Mississauga, Ontario. Distributed in
Australia by Millennium Books, 13/3 Maddox Street, Alexandria NSW 2015.
Distributed in New Zealand by Tandem Press, 2 Rugby Road, Birkenhead,
Auckland 10. Distributed in the United Kingdom by Verulam Publishing,
Ltd., 152a Park Street Lane, Park Street, St. Albans, Hertfordshire AL2 2AU.

ISBN 1-55853-386-9

Printed in the United States of America
1 2 3 4 5 6 7 8 9—99 98 97 96 95

Introduction

William F. Buckley Jr.

The irradiations were felt everywhere, felt by people who liked Newt Gingrich and by people who didn't like him; and, pretty soon, by people who hadn't known whether they liked him or not—because they didn't even know who or what he was. Mr. Bentley's camera appears to have sensed this, because in these photographs we have a folio of an arrival in American history. Maybe Newt Gingrich will go on one day (soon, or later) to be president, and it's true that the special majesty in American politics attaches only to the president. But the Speaker of the House is the foreman of the factory, and whatever the president of the company says, sweetly or clangorously, he is going to get what the factory produces. Newt Gingrich found himself, on November 8, 1994, the new Speaker of the House, the first Republican to occupy that post in 40 years. And he was armed with what he insisted was a mandate from the electorate.

What was *that* all about? His Contract with America. It listed 10 legislative objectives to which he pledged himself, and which he asked every Republican incumbent and every Republican candidate for a seat in the House to endorse. They did so and when the voters gave them the majority vote, Newt (yes, there isn't any idiomatic way of avoiding this simple one-syllable name by which he is everywhere known) announced that this wasn't like a routine political victory, it was a victory with a prewritten script, ranging from a balanced budget to term limitations.

Mr. Bentley has caught this, what one might call the reification of a figure who will be lodged in American history books. I remember reading about the phenomenon at Hyannis Port on November 9, 1960, at the summer compound of the Kennedy family. That tense morning it was crowded with photographers and television cameras and reporters. They had followed Jack Kennedy for weeks, some of them for months, and the climax was at hand. It was a race so close that the votes in one city (Chicago) and one state (Texas) had made the difference. Some time after midnight, it gradually crystallized that John Fitzgerald Kennedy would be the next president of the United States.

What caught this eye was the appearance of Kennedy at eight in the morning. He stepped into the large room where the press were seated, some on the floor. They were all familiar to him, indeed most of them referred to him as "Jack." But at that moment, at that hour, they rose spontaneously to their feet.

The historical moment suggests itself. It's pretty obvious when dealing with presidents who are elected or kings who die. But for offices, however exalted, of the second rank, something else is required, and that has been captured adroitly by Mr. Bentley in this book. A personal magnetism. The easiest way to say it is that Newt Gingrich generates excitement.

What is it that makes this happen? Certainly not his face, which is forgettable: Bentley shows us Gingrich before his great day, riding the subway, nobody bothering to look at him. Certainly not his clothes. Murray Kempton, describing the late Senator Joe McCarthy, once wrote that he looked as if he was wearing a suit that had been washed in clam chowder. Well, Newt isn't *that* disheveled, but one does get the idea, reinforced in several photographs here, that shopping for clothes is done by relaying to the department store the three or four relevant coordinates of his body size. His voice? It is on the high side, and every now and again one thinks one is hearing a whinny . . .

So? Well, just to begin with, Gingrich is very intelligent. He is very well read. He is utterly at home with the benefits of tradition, which he seeks to preserve, and meanwhile quivers with excitement over what lies ahead. He has confessed his romance with cyberspace, but it is unaffected by his reverence for a Constitution written over two hundred years ago. And the briskness of his walk (observe him climbing the Capitol steps) keeps reminding us of his anxiety to get on with it.

Get on with what?

Gingrich captures the imagination by suggesting that he has an idea of what has gone wrong with America. Most Americans aren't making better money than they were when Richard Nixon was in office. There are signs of the malaise to which Jimmy Carter referred during his term in office. Something stalled. The economy? The accretions on the economy, weighed down by debt, military overhead, social services?

Yes, says Gingrich—the same man who credited Franklin Delano Roosevelt as a great president when giving his inaugural address as Speaker. He does believe there are barriers to the revitalization of a genuine recovery. But he is not of the school that believes those barriers are geological in character, as unmovable as great glaciers and ocean floors. He has ideas on how to rekindle the American idea, and Mr. Bentley, if his camera were equipped with an X ray, would no doubt have captured the fire in Newt's belly.

Permit my prejudices to show here: I am addicted to black-and-white photography, and designed one hundred covers of *National Review,* in years gone by, with the black-and-white photographs of Jan Lukas. Bentley has a sense of the occasion, which is obvious, an eye for structure and an exuberant confidence that he will give us in black and white not something as good as color, but something better. And the tabloid feel of many of these pictures reflects the mood of the book, which is of a great American event in very rapid process: the arrival of a figure unknown yesterday, obsessively familiar today. Oh, there are plenty of photos of Gingrich in offices, Gingrich in conversation, Gingrich reflecting, one or two even reading. But the sense of motion is that of an athletic event, a high diver who has miles to go before he lands.

Five weeks after engineering the most stunning congressional election upset in decades, Newt Gingrich is still a figure so unknown to most Americans that he can ride the subway (*previous page*) and do his Christmas shopping without causing much of a stir. The everyday luxuries of obscurity wouldn't last much longer.

Previous page: The Speaker-to-be arrives in Washington the day before he will hold the gavel for the first time. Still unaccustomed to the perquisites that come with his new job, he has a bit of trouble locating his car and driver at the airport.

Gingrich puts the finishing touches on the first speech that he will give as Speaker (*right*). In the House Chamber, only a few yards away from his ceremonial office, the roll is being called in the election that will formally make Gingrich the first Republican to lead the House in four decades.

To jubilant chants of "Newt! Newt!" Gingrich takes the final steps in a most unlikely 16-year journey. A man who made his reputation as a troublemaker in the back benches now commands the podium.

"I am very fortunate. . . . Sometimes when you get to be my age, you cannot have everyone near you that you would like to have. I cannot say how much I learned from my dad and his years of serving in the U.S. Army and how much I learned from my mother, who is clearly my most enthusiastic cheerleader."

The day's jubilation was marred by a small furor: in an interview on national television, CBS's Connie Chung had coaxed Gingrich's mother into whispering derogatory comments about First Lady Hillary Rodham Clinton. Here, Kit Gingrich gets a hug and a word of consolation from her son.

Following page: At a celebration that evening, the new Speaker addresses a crowd of well-wishers. Breaking with tradition, Gingrich had put the House to work on its opening day. The opening session saw more than 600 bills formally introduced in the House, but the first 100 days would be tightly focused on implementing the 10 promises of the Republicans' Contract with America.

"*It may be more than a decade before the forces that have been set in motion achieve their full result. But most students of American history would agree that another era of American reform has begun.*"

After a 14 1/2-hour session that was as gruelling as it was euphoric, the Speaker celebrates the passage of the nine measures overhauling the way the House does business. Former Press Secretary Rich Galen (*below,* at left), drops by to share a laugh with his successor, Tony Blankley (at center), along with Gingrich and political consultant Joe Gaylord. Later in the evening, the Speaker is joined by two of his oldest allies— Pennsylvania congressman Bob Walker (*left,* at left) and Connie Mack, a Florida senator.

Hillary Rodham Clinton (*left*) puts an embarrassing episode to rest by hosting Gingrich and his mother on a private tour of the White House. Meanwhile, the Speaker becomes accustomed to finding camera crews everywhere he goes—even outside his Capitol Hill apartment.

"The scientific and technological changes going on around us are far more significant than we have recognized. If we can grasp the true significance of these changes, we can lead the world into the Information Age and leave our children a country unmatched in wealth, power, and opportunity."

"Ideas matter." Running a revolution would seem to be a full-time job. But Gingrich also wrote two books, hosted a weekly cable television show, and returned to Georgia every Saturday morning to teach a college course entitled "Renewing American Civilization." Here, he addresses a conference hosted by the Progress & Freedom Foundation (*left*), which sponsored his show and televised course. Futurists Alvin and Heidi Toffler (*below*) are part of his eclectic circle of advisers.

"I don't see anything wrong with the idea that there's a creative tension between the House and the Senate, between the legislative and the executive, and the Supreme Court is there watching all of us and protecting constitutional liberties."

Less than two weeks after the Republicans took over, the Speaker was driving the agenda in Washington. He commands center stage while meeting with a delegation of New York state officials (*below*), and even on President Clinton's turf (*right*) during a strategy session on Mexico's economic crisis.

Gingrich's footsteps echo many times each day in the Capitol's
ornate statuary hall (*above*), which lies between the House
Chamber and his office (*right*).

The Speaker and Senate Majority Leader Bob Dole (*right*) confer before a news conference celebrating their first joint achievement—requiring Congress to live under the labor laws it passes for everyone else. Later that day, amid uproar over their book deal, Gingrich and media baron Rupert Murdoch (*below,* at left) find themselves together at a House GOP dinner for telecommunications executives.

Following page: Seeking to quiet the controversy, Gingrich reminds reporters that he has agreed to give up a $4.5-million book advance, accepting only $1, plus royalties. The questions continued. Ultimately, he abandoned the regular news conferences entirely.

As they await President Clinton's arrival in the House Chamber for his annual State of the Union Address, Gingrich and Vice President Al Gore survey the crowd in the galleries to find the Speaker's wife, Marianne. Later that week, Gingrich confers with one of his most trusted lieutenants, Ohio congressman John Boehner (*right*), the blunt-spoken chairman of the Republican Conference.

Gingrich describes House Majority Leader Dick Armey as his "chief operating officer," though Armey's choice in footwear is hardly boardroom issue (*left*). Steve Hanser (*below*), the older brother figure who has been Gingrich's chief sounding board since their days together as college professors, plays that role again during the Speaker's stint as a classroom lecturer. Hanser also gave the future leader of the House his first taste of political defeat by beating him in his 1972 bid to become chairman of the West Georgia College history department.

Following page: The Speaker, Tipper Gore (at center), and singer-turned-congressman Sonny Bono (at far right) are among the celebrities attending the annual Washington Press Club Foundation dinner.

Giddily trying to get the Speaker's attention, Budget Committee
Chairman John Kasich (*left*), with Don Fierce, a strategist with the
Republican National Committee, taps on the window of his office.
Fierce and RNC Chairman Haley Barbour (*below*) provided
crucial advice and support to the House Republican agenda.

Following page: With a giant electronic image of the Speaker
hovering specterlike over their heads, members of the American
Hospital Association train their attention on the real thing
onstage. Never had the speakership of the House proven to be a
pulpit of such bully proportions, or a platform that could rival the
White House.

Technology buff Gingrich addresses the Cellular Telephone
Industry from a Republican National Committee studio near the
Capitol (*above*). Although Gingrich's Republicans presented a
public image of near-unanimity, the monumental task of
producing a balanced budget created many strains in private.
Meeting with members of his leadership team, the Speaker
emphasizes the need to work together (*right*).

"If all the pro-term-limits, anti-tax-increase, decentralize-government, shrink-the-bureaucracy folks stay together as one party, we will win a smashing victory in '96, and it will be a victory for those values."

"In nearly all countries, power belongs to the state and is occasionally loaned to individuals. In America, power comes from God to the individual and is loaned to the state. . . . It would be hard to imagine a greater difference in first principles."

While Vice President Gore offers an invocation at the National Prayer Breakfast, the Speaker joins in prayer backstage. Later that day, Gingrich surprises his wife, Marianne, by dropping in on her at lunch.

Following page: Gingrich aides John Duncan, Dan Meyer, and Arne Christenson show their boss their budget plan for the rest of the fiscal year.

Having previously focused almost exclusively on domestic matters, the new Speaker found himself called upon to make regular pronouncements on foreign policy—an area where he felt decidedly less certain of himself. "I'm still learning," he admitted. Here, he meets with Israeli Foreign Minister Shimon Peres. That evening, he was back to national politics, appearing at a televised "town meeting" (*right*).

Following page: The Speaker helps his wife get her suitcases out the door of their Capitol Hill apartment building as she heads for Israel, where she does business development for a private firm.

By his February appearance at a Republican National Committee dinner, Gingrich was able to boast that the House had passed half the items in the Contract with America. Though their relationship had been a testy one over the years, Gingrich and Dole (*above*) understood that their political destinies were now tied. Republican governors such as California's Pete Wilson (*right,* at left) and Michigan's John Engler (at center) also found themselves newly influential with a Congress determined to send power back to the states.

Following page: A green carnation in his lapel, Gingrich escorts Clinton up the Capitol steps for a St. Patrick's Day luncheon.

"We have to go out and establish hope. For all these years we were the party of anger, we were the party of despair, we were the party stopping big government. We are not anymore. We are the party liberating the American people."

Stress and exhaustion often gave way to silliness among Gingrich's top aides: Len Swinehart (*left*), whose job it is to ensure that Gingrich gets no surprises on the House floor; Arne Christenson (*below*, at left), Gingrich's top budget staffer; and Budget Committee Chairman John Kasich (at right), who can claim the distinction of having been the only congressman ever evicted from the stage of a Grateful Dead concert.

Following page: In his zeal to cut the budget, the irrepressible Kasich (at center) often stepped on the turf and the egos of other committee chairmen. It was left to Gingrich to tell his protégé when he had gone too far.

Almost always present at critical moments, Joe Gaylord (*below,* at left) is the Speaker's chief political strategist and perhaps his most trusted adviser. "There are a lot more layers to me" than most people understand, Gingrich says. "Other than Hanser and Gaylord and my wife, I don't think anybody bridges all of them." The tabloids, meanwhile, suggest that Gingrich is reaching into space for advice.

Following page: The Speaker finds himself, for once, outside the focus of attention as he waits to speak at a news conference celebrating the midpoint of the House Republicans' first 100 days.

"Our fear was that seventy-five eager freshmen would arrive in Washington, walk around in dazed happiness for a few months, then slowly be taken into the fold by lobbyists, media personalities, and the rest of the Washington establishment. That would have been worse than losing the election."

Halfway through the first 100 days, the Republicans had yet to tackle some of the more difficult items on their agenda: setting term limits, cutting taxes, and reforming welfare. At weekly Republicans-only meetings in the House Chamber, the Speaker tries to keep them on track.

Following page: Exhaustion shows at yet another budget session with Christenson.

Republicans made their first major public-relations blunder when they moved to curb the growth of the school lunch program. With the Democrats on the attack, defining a clear message on the budget took on new urgency. Kasich's press secretary, Bruce Cuthbertson (*left,* at far left), has a word with his boss during one of the endless budget strategy sessions consuming the Republicans' days. Armey confers with Jack Howard (*above,* at left), a special assistant to the Speaker.

Following page: As the pace picked up in the House, so did the demands for appearances by the man in charge of the revolution. Here, Gingrich speaks to the National Restaurant Association.

*"I'm a very aggressive, risk-taking person. . . .
But as Speaker, styles and patterns that made
perfect sense when I was the Whip are irrational.
Imagine yourself a stage actor with the size of
gestures you need to be seen in the back row. And
now you become a large-screen movie actor."*

Rachel Robinson and Anne Beighey (*below*) were responsible for keeping Gingrich as close to his schedule as possible. Whenever their cheerful miens turned serious, the Speaker would know it was time to wrap up one meeting, such as this session with Irish students, and move on to the next.

"A country whose children can't read, a country where 12-year-olds have babies and 15-year-olds kill each other and 17-year-olds die of AIDS is not a country that's going to lead anybody. If we're going to fulfill our duty to the human race, we have to fulfill our duty here at home."

One of the endeavors of which Gingrich was most proud was his involvement in the "Earning by Learning" program. Disadvantaged children, such as these at Moten Elementary in Washington, D.C., earn money for reading as many as 80 books in a summer.

The Speaker's favorite adviser on foreign policy is Henry Kissinger (*above*). However, his leadership team—including (*right, top to bottom*) Deputy Whip Dennis Hastert, Chief of Staff Meyer, and House Majority Leader Armey—finds itself stumped over how to handle Mexico's economic crisis after the Speaker's support for a bailout ignited rebellion among his troops.

Following page: Family affairs again become national ones when the Speaker's lesbian half-sister Candace (at far right) meets with the brother whose policies she has criticized. Another half-sister, Robbie Brown, joins them to take a bit of the edge off the event.

"America is too big, too diverse, and too free to be run by bureaucrats sitting in office buildings in one city. . . . We simply must shift power and responsibility back to state governments, local governments, nonprofit institutions, and—most important of all—individual citizens."

With an overhaul of federal regulations under debate, Chief of Staff Meyer (*left*, at left), Floor Assistant Jay Pierson, and Deputy Press Secretary Lauren Sims brief Gingrich on what to expect from the media that day.

Two of Gingrich's favorite props (*above*) are a vacuum tube and a computer chip, symbolizing how far technology has come. Discussing a more pressing and controversial matter, the Speaker tries to quell the dissent that is brewing among Republican factions over term limits (*right*). The issue would become the one proposal in the Contract with America that failed to pass the House.

Following page: Veterans, who form one of the most powerful lobbies on Capitol Hill, plead their case with the Speaker. A week later, the House would handily defeat an effort to cut $206 million from veterans' health care.

"It is hard to lead a free people; in many ways it is much easier to get the job done by simply allowing a bureaucracy to tell people what to do. Yet in the long run, the strength of a free society is the commitment of every person to solve real problems and bear real responsibility."

Springtime gave the Speaker more opportunities to move his work onto his beloved balcony. Here, he confers with Press Secretary Tony Blankley (at left) and Chief of Staff Meyer, with the ever-vigilant Rachel Robinson standing watch in the background.

Following page: At the Radio-T.V. Correspondents Association Annual Dinner, which featured a speech by President Clinton, the Speaker leaves his tuxedo at home. Having spent much of his career courting the media, Gingrich now frequently found himself at odds with the press corps. "I think an awful lot of reporters don't get the scale of the change yet, although we're winning some tactical skirmishes," he said.

"I think the Rings Trilogy by Tolkien caught it perfectly. Any of us who carries the ring of power is weakened inevitably to some extent by its possession. Any of us runs the risk of corruption. And anyone who thinks they don't misunderstands their own humanness."

In mid-March, a crucial spending-cut bill became entangled in issues that ranged from abortion to taxes. With the bill in jeopardy, so was the Republicans' credibility. For the first time, their public show of unity gave way to widespread and open squabbling within the ranks. At strategy sessions, Gingrich's annoyance is obvious.

"This is a real revolution. In real revolutions, the defeated faction doesn't tend to convert, it tends to go down fighting."

On the eve of the vote on the $17.4-billion cut in federal spending, Appropriations Committee Chairman Bob Livingston (*left*) makes an impassioned appeal for solidarity during a private meeting of Republicans. Armey and Gingrich meet with Rules Committee Chairman Gerald Solomon (*following page,* at center) to plot their strategy for keeping the welfare reform bill intact on the House floor. After initial difficulties, both bills passed.

"As Eisenhower taught over and over, leading a coalition involves listening to your allies more than lecturing them, and learning from your allies more than teaching them."

A Jordanian delegation led by King Hussein and Queen Noor meets with Gingrich in his office (*left*). At an Irish pub on Capitol Hill (*above*), the Gingriches partake in a less regal celebration of the passage of the welfare bill.

The Contract's last item, a middle-class tax cut, proved a closer call than expected. Meyer, Gingrich, Whip Tom DeLay, and Deputy Whip Hastert (*above*) nervously count votes. With five hours to go, they were still 10 short. Yet as Gingrich confidently steps onto the House floor for the daily opening rituals (*right*), he betrays no sign of the difficulties behind the scenes.

Miguel Davis, a 10-year-old aspiring photographer (*below*), gets his first professional experience snapping Gingrich with a group of visitors. At the request of House Republicans, Chris Farley of *Saturday Night Live* surprises the Speaker (*right*) by appearing at a GOP meeting and doing his Newt imitation.

"Americans as a people have the natural ability to respond to change. That is what we do best when the government is not in the way."

As a child, Gingrich aspired to be a zookeeper—which, by some measures, is not much of a leap from the job he now has. Among the visitors he entertains at the Capitol are a bearcat from the Columbus Zoo and a troupe of elephants from the Ringling Brothers and Barnum & Bailey Circus. As the Republicans drew near to completing their 100 days of reform, the elephants parading through Capitol Plaza provided a hefty note of symbolism.

Gingrich ended his historic 100 days with celebration and reflection. As the day begins, he polishes the speech he will deliver that evening (*left*), which outlined what he planned to do next, and then joins Blankley (*below*) in scanning the assessments that the media is making of the First Hundred Days.

Following pages: Jubilant House Republicans declare: "Promises made; promises kept" at a ceremony on the Capitol steps—the site where only 6½ months before they had signed their 10-point Contract with America. At the time, it had been dismissed as a campaign gimmick; it proved to be a blueprint for governing.

"It is in the spirit of committing ourselves idealistically, committing ourselves romantically, believing in America, that we celebrate having kept our word. And we promise to begin a new partnership, so that together we and the American people can give our children and our country a new birth of freedom."

Gingrich capped off his 100-day triumph with an unprecedented, presidential-style address, broadcast from his office balcony (*left*). The celebrations over, he carries books and papers home for a three-week break from the relentless pace. It is 1:35 A.M. when the exhausted Gingriches collapse on the couch of their apartment (*following page*).

NEW HAMPSHIRE

SUNDAY NEWS

SHOWDOWN

Clinton and Gingrich Agree to a Granite State

Was Gingrich's June trip to New Hampshire the beginning of a presidential campaign? The press treated it as if it were, but the Speaker denied it, claiming he had only come to see a moose. In the midst of the media circus, Gaylord ponders the headline declaring a "showdown" (*left*) between Gingrich and Clinton. Marianne gives her husband a kiss of encouragement (*below*) before he joins the President in what proves to be an amiable joint appearance (*following page*).

Quotations from the Writings and Speeches of Speaker Newt Gingrich

Page 20 "Inaugural Address." Speech given by the Speaker of the House to the House of Representatives, Washington, D.C., January 4, 1995.

Page 22 *To Renew America*. (New York: HarperCollins Publishers, 1995), p.6.

Page 29 *To Renew America*. p. 7.

Page 30 1995. Interview with Bob Schieffer. "Face the Nation." CBS, 9, April.

Page 49 1995. Interview with Bob Schieffer. "Face the Nation." CBS, 9, April.

Page 51 *To Renew America*. p.34.

Page 59 "Speech to the Republican National Committee." Address given by the Speaker of the House to the Republican National Committee, Washington, D.C., January 20, 1995.

Page 69 *To Renew America*. p.115.

Page 77 1995. Interview by David Frost. "Talking with David Frost." Public Broadcasting Service, 31, March.

Page 80 "An American Vision for the 21st Century." Address given by the Speaker of the House at policy conference held at the Nixon Center, Washington, D.C., March 1, 1995.

Page 87 *To Renew America*. p. 9.

Page 92 *To Renew America*. p. 105.

Page 97 1995. Interview by David Frost. "Talking with David Frost." Public Broadcasting Service, 31, March.

Page 99 "Speech to the Republican National Committee." Address given by the Speaker of the House to the Republican National Committee, Washington, D.C., January 20, 1995.

Page 102 "An American Vision for the 21st Century." Address given by the Speaker of the House at policy conference held at the Nixon Center, Washington, D.C., March 1, 1995.

Page 108 "Address to the Nation." Address given by the Speaker of the House to a national television audience, Washington, D.C., April 7, 1995.

Page 117 "Address to the Nation." Address given by the Speaker of the House to a national television audience, Washington, D.C., April 7, 1995.

Acknowledgments

This project could not have been done without the cooperation of Newt Gingrich. He and Marianne were able to open up their lives to me and make me feel like an old friend. Thanks are not enough to express my gratitude.

This journalistic journey also could not have been made without the financial and editorial support of TIME magazine's Managing Editor Jim Gaines, Picture Editor Michele Stephenson, and Nation Picture Editor Rick Boeth. Particular kudos and sympathy to Rick for having to look at every frame I shot!

To Gingrich Press Secretary Tony Blankley, thanks for your jovial *savior faire* and help over the 100 days.

Thanks to the entire Republican House for allowing me into their world for this period and ignoring me in all the meetings and on the House floor. Special memo to House Majority Leader Dick Armey: Great boots, Tex!

To Senate Majority Leader Bob Dole, thank you for letting me be a fly on the wall in your offices, as well.

My gratitude to Bill Livingood, the House Sergeant at Arms, for helping open some doors that had previously been closed to me.

To the Speaker's entire staff, thanks so much for all your help in making the 100 days fun. Particular recognition to Dan Meyer, Lauren Sims, Leigh Ann Metzger, John Cox, and Robert George. Also, a big thanks to the Speaker's detail of the Capitol Hill Police for their professionalism and courtesy.

To Hardy Lott, I really appreciated your Southern hospitality and Fig *Newt*ons.

And to Rachel Robinson and Anne Beighey, with whom I spent many a day in Newt's office, thanks for your good cheer, information, laughs, and schedules.

To my colleagues in the press corps who cover the Hill, my gratitude for your support and advice during the 100 days.

Finally to Beth, thanks for enduring the cold to be with me.

Gotta go . . . surf's up and I'm catching that fourth wave! Aloha, P.F.

All photographs for this book were taken with
Leica and Canon cameras on Kodak Tri-X and P-3200 film.

Typeset in Times Roman using QuarkXPress 3.3
software on Macintosh computers.

Photographic printing by
Grace Zaccardi, Baltimore, Maryland.

Duotone separations and film output by
Capitol Engraving Co., Nashville, Tennessee.

Printing by R.R. Donnelley & Sons, Willard, Ohio.